THE COCKTAIL GUIDE TO THE GALAXY

ALSO BY ME WHEN I WAS GOING
UNDER THE PEN NAME R. ANDREW HEIDEL

Beyond the Wall of Sleep
Desperate Moon: Three Collections

A Universe
of Unique Cocktails
from the Celebrated
Doctor Who Bar

THE COCKTAIL GUIDE TO THE GALAXY

ANDY HEIDEL

 ST. MARTIN'S GRIFFIN ≈ NEW YORK

For the Ambassadors, Space Friends, and other
regulars of The Way Station . . . and thirsty nerds everywhere

THE COCKTAIL GUIDE TO THE GALAXY. Copyright © 2017 by Richard Andrew Heidel. All rights reserved. Printed in the United States of America. For information, address St. Martin's Press, 175 Fifth Avenue, New York, NY 10010.

www.stmartins.com

Designed by Anna Gorovoy

The Library of Congress Cataloging-in-Publication Data is available upon request.

ISBN 978-1-250-12121-9 (hardcover)
ISBN 978-1-250-12122-6 (ebook)

Our books may be purchased in bulk for promotional, educational, or business use. Please contact your local bookseller or the Macmillan Corporate and Premium Sales Department at 1-800-221-7945, extension 5442, or by email at MacmillanSpecialMarkets@macmillan.com.

First Edition: September 2017

10 9 8 7 6 5 4 3 2 1

WARNING

All cocktails contained within this book have been field-tested by some of the best bartenders in Brooklyn, the most amazing regulars at TWS, and also some random people who just happened to be at the bar when I was inspired to invent a cocktail. This book has been rated MA for strong drinks and language.

The Geek shall inherit the Earth.

CONTENTS

HIGHLANDER

THE HITCHHIKER'S GUIDE TO THE GALAXY

THE HUNGER GAMES

INDIANA JONES

INVASION OF THE BODY SNATCHERS

JURASSIC PARK

LOST IN SPACE

LORD OF THE RINGS

THE MARTIAN

MAD MAX

THE MATRIX

MEN IN BLACK

METROPOLIS

MYSTERY SCIENCE THEATER 3000

Hawkins: The pellet with the poison's in the flagon with the dragon; the vessel with the pestle has the brew that is true.
Griselda: Just remember that.

 —*The Court Jester,* 1955

Kirk: Know anything about the radiation surge?
Chekov: Only the size of my head.
Kirk: I know what you mean.

 —*Star Trek VI: The Undiscovered Country,* 1991

FOREWORD: ALL OF THIS WILL MAKE SENSE TO YOU SOON, I PROMISE

BY CHLOÉ SEHR

Let's be very clear about one thing: when I walk into The Way Station, the bar that my friend Anders owns, I HAVE NO IDEA WHAT ANYONE IS TALKING ABOUT. I have many friends there who are wonderful people. We have great conversations about the events of the day, we gripe about New York the way New Yorkers do. Then, someone makes a reference to any one of a zillion sci-fi films/TV shows/comic books and they may as well be speaking Swahili, as far as I'm concerned.

It's possible I would never have wandered into The Way Station at all, if not for the fact that Anders is my best friend. We met years ago when we were both bartenders at a restaurant in the neighborhood. He was already trying to open The Way Station, a grueling two-year process that is a story for another day. Luckily, our boss was an excellent example of what not to do as an employer, which drove Anders to draft pages and pages of helpful suggestions. Even though they fell on deaf ears (blind eyes?) then, I'm quite sure he has implemented all of those ideas in running things at his own bar to this very day. Smart man, our Anders.

Since The Way Station opened in 2011, Anders has created a home for folks who love the stuff he loves and I know nothing about—Doctor

Who, *Star Trek,* comic books, sexy science lectures, superheroes, et cetera. The list goes on and on and on. In fact, he has even opened his actual home to various friends he's made there over the years. How many times have I wandered out of our shared office in the spare room of his apartment to find some lovely, bespectacled woman in the living room, quietly watching (what I now know is) Doctor Who on Anders's television and commented, "Ooh, look! R2D2!" only to have her whirl around and shriek, "THAT'S NOT R2D2! THAT'S NOT R2D2!" Ah, yes. Such is the passion and dedication to all things science fiction that is the bedrock of The Way Station and its success.

So now that I've clearly delineated why I'm unqualified to speak about the theme of this book, why should you listen to me and buy one for yourself and then buy a copy for every single person you know and love? Exactly. This book of cocktails, like its author, like The Way Station, has a curious yet universal and undeniable appeal. I don't know what or who a Gollum is, but you bet I'd try a My Precious. Why? Because it's weird and sounds delicious and the drawing that goes with it is really cool. Because this book is so cleverly written and entertaining that I can't put it down. Because, when you read this book, you will realize, like I did so many years ago, somewhere in the drunken wee hours at The Way Station, that you don't have to know what that big blue box in the corner is to have a good time here. Trust me.

THE COCKTAIL GUIDE TO THE GALAXY

READY PLAYER ONE

Most cocktail books start with a gauntlet of glassware, intimidating accoutrements, and technical terms to craft the perfect cocktail. This isn't that type of book. The recipes you are about to follow are simple, but the results are delicious, and hopefully I will entertain and educate you along the way. You are holding this book because you like to drink and I like to make drinks. I also like to drink.

I don't expect you to run out and buy shakers, stirrers, strainers, or specialty glassware. Use what you got. If the only thing clean in your cupboard is a jelly jar, go for it. You might not have a jigger but you probably have measuring cups or spoons, a soda bottle cap, table spoons, or a spork. Also, if you don't have a long spoon, chopsticks work just as well for stirring. Making drinks is supposed to be fun. Drinking them? Even more fun.

In order to simplify the drink-making process, I'll talk about "parts." One part is 1 1/2 ounces, but hey, if you're having a party and want to make a batch, one part could be a liter of vodka, then you can use the empty bottle as a measuring tool for the other parts and add the extras (dashes and splashes) to taste.

As for ingredients, I'll use a brand name if it makes sense for the cocktail name or flavor, but I'll offer alternatives if you don't have that brand or KHAAAAAAN't find it.

So, whether you want to toast your enemies with Klingon Blood Wine or take your chances with the Pan Galactic Gargle Blaster (and wake up feeling like your brain got smashed out with a gold brick wrapped in a lemon peel), this is the book for you, or your wonderfully nerdy/geeky thirsty friend.

MAKING DRINKS THAT MAKE SENSE

One of the most enjoyable aspects of my job is creating new cocktails. Sometimes it starts with a name like "Captain Jack" from *Doctor Who* and *Torchwood* (page 71), which immediately reveals the ingredients *Captain* Morgan's and *Jack* Daniel's, both of which are traditionally mixed with Coca-Cola. Voilà, a cocktail.

Sometimes there's a traditional cocktail that lends itself easily to becoming a new drink. For example, the classic screwdriver (orange juice and vodka) becomes a Doctor Who sonic screwdriver when you add a colorful cordial. Ta-da!

Sometimes a drink gets its name after the fact. I once had a customer ask me for a delicious gin drink so I muddled cucumber and added gin and grapefruit and cranberry juice. She drank six of them and was a train wreck afterward, hence the name (see page 161, under *Snow-piercer*).

There is also the quest. Years ago I was served a Rocky Mountain Motherfucker. I thought it was a popular drink. It wasn't. Nobody outside of the Victorian Lady in Willimantic, Connecticut, knew how to make it. Once I started bartending I endeavored to re-create it via taste memory, and after many tipsy nights I finally succeeded. I have renamed this holy grail of cocktails in this book as the Awesome Mixed Drink (page 111).

Finally, there is the challenge. One day, a regular at the bar asked me to make him a reason to live so that he could ask for one after a rough day. I gave it a shot on the fly, but it wasn't good enough. Disappointed that I failed him, I spent the next month trying out different and unique cocktails and eventually hit upon the right combination of sweet, salty, bitter, and sour in the right proportions; it was delicious in a savory way akin to umami, the fifth taste. The cocktail was a hit and definitely made a difference in my customer's day when he ordered it. I repurposed that recipe in this book for my *Fifth Element* cocktail, Divinian (page 89).

INSTRUCTIONS FOR MAKING THE DRINKS CONTAINED HEREIN

Simple

1) Get a glass.
2) Fill it with ice.
3) Add all ingredients except anything bubbly.
4) Stir, shake, or pour from glass to glass to chill your cocktail fast.
5) If you don't want your drink to get diluted, strain out the ice while pouring into another glass.
6) Add any ingredients that contain bubbles last.

Advanced

Fill your preferred drinking vessel with ice water before making your drink. Mix your drink in another vessel. Once the cocktail is mixed, empty your chilled drinking vessel and strain the cocktail into it.

Ultra-super-complicated advanced cocktails that will make you want to find a safe space

Just kidding. I will have specific instructions for making these special cocktails work.

Splash = 1/8 part or 1 wedge of citrus

Glassware

We covered this earlier, but we need a place to work from. Since you might not have a coupe, collins, highball, pint, martini, or flute, I will suggest a small glass (4-ounce, like a rocks), medium glass (10- to 12-ounce, like a collins), big glass (14- to 16-ounce, like a pint), or fancy glass (4- to 6-ounce, like a wine, Champagne, coupe, or martini) for serving. As we work in parts, this will ensure that even if you use a giant pickle jar as your vessel, your cocktail will still be crafted perfectly.

Idiot-proofing

My best friend Chloé said no one would read this section and would just skip right to the drinks. So just in case she's right, every cocktail has specific instructions.

We are all about improvising in this Omniverse.

One part is 1 1/2 ounces (50 ml) and is equivalent to 3 tablespoons.

WHY THE WAY STATION?

Once upon a time, I dreamed of being a writer. Instead, I ended up a publicist at Avon Books working with my literary heroes—Neal Stephenson, Ray Bradbury, Neil Gaiman, and Terry Pratchett. I was in heaven. That was followed by another dream job working at the Sci-Fi Channel (before it became Syfy, WTF, seriously?) publicizing *Farscape, Dune,* J. Michael Straczynski, and Adam West. I published two collections of short stories and sold a script to Roger Corman, but never made a living off my writing. Years and jobs later, I got downsized at the start of the 2008 recession.

I was broke, on unemployment, and depressed. Every job interview I went on led to the same conclusion: hiring freeze. Eventually I got a part-time job tending bar at a restaurant on Vanderbilt Avenue in Prospect Heights, Brooklyn, and discovered that many of our patrons would come from a few blocks away on Washington Avenue, where there weren't many bars or restaurants at the time. I had an idea that was obvious: open a bar where there was a need for one and no competition. I borrowed from my family and friends, maxed out my credit cards, and built The Way Station.

As a first-time bar owner, I wasn't familiar with building codes. Evidently, you need something called a "certificate of occupancy" stating that you are properly zoned as an eating and drinking establishment in order to obtain your liquor license in New York City. My building was zoned as retail. All of a sudden I needed an architect to draw plans, a certified plumber to redo my work, and files and forms to be approved by the Department of Buildings. Weeks stretched into months, months into years. My friends were losing faith. Some of them started calling my bar "Two Weeks" because I was always that close to opening when something else would go wrong. Twenty-one months after I signed the lease, I finally got my certificate of occupancy, picked up my liquor license, borrowed two thousand dollars from my sister to buy supplies, and opened up that night. The bar was packed. Succeeding after such a long struggle was an incredible relief and total joy. Now, years later, I'm writing this cocktail book for people like me: nerds who like to celebrate their fandom in whatever way they can. In my case—this book.

MOVING FORWARD

After six years of running TWS, the one constant is that many of our first-time patrons don't know how to behave in a bar. For you, my soon-to-be customers, friends, and bargoers, I will share some "Heidel Hints" and "Anders Anecdotes" to instruct you on your drinking career. At The Way Station you will be treated well, no matter what, unless you have sex in the bathroom, creep on women, or are generally an asshole. This instructional advice is for you occasional bargoers so that you may navigate a great night out.

12 MONKEYS

12-Step Monkey
ILLUSTRATION BY ED REYNOLDS

WE:

1. *Admitted we gain power from alcohol—that without it our lives are unimaginable.*
2. *Came to believe that Powers whiskey is greater than ourselves and can restore us to sanity.*
3. *Made a decision to turn our will and our livers over to the care of the bartender.*
4. *Made a searching and fearless moral inventory of who at the bar was willing to listen to us, and from whom we might get that phone number.*
5. *Admitted to the bartender, to ourselves, and to another human being at the bar the exact nature of our wrongs, rights, and pipe dreams.*
6. *Were entirely ready to have the bartender remove us from the bar if we behaved badly.*

7. *Humbly asked the bartender to point out our shortcomings.*
8. *Made a list of all persons we had upset or wronged, real or imaginary, and became willing to make amends to them all by buying them a round of drinks.*
9. *Made direct amends to such people, wherever possible, with a hug and a toast, except when to do so would injure them or others.*
10. *Continued to take personal inventory (phone, wallet, ID, credit card, coat, bag) and when we were missing items, promptly admitted it, asked the bartender for help, and tipped generously.*
11. *Sought through tips and toasts to improve our conscious contact with the bartender, praying only for knowledge and a shot of Powers to carry that out.*
12. *Having had a drunken experience as the result of these steps, we tried to carry this message to other bargoers, barflies, and regulars, and to practice these principles in all our affairs.*

1 part Powers whiskey
1/4 part Cointreau or triple sec
Splash lemon juice
1 monkey (optional)

Pour all the ingredients into a small glass filled with ice. Stir. Imbibe in your favorite time-traveling chair.

2001: A SPACE ODYSSEY

HAL

ILLUSTRATION BY ELIZABETH DAGGAR

The problem with artificial intelligence, much like artificial sweeteners, is that eventually they will kill you. This homicidal drink's acronym gives us a clue to the ingredients within.

1 part Hpnotiq
1/4 part Aperol
Splash of lemon juice

Pour all the ingredients into a small glass filled with ice. Stir. Garnish with lies and a maraschino cherry (kinda looks like HAL's eye).

After one sip you'll say, "My god, it's full of bars." Drink until your speech slurs while singing "Daisy" to yourself.

Pod Bay Breeze

This chilling concoction based on the classic Bay Breeze will ease those second thoughts about your mission.

1 part Cognac
1 part cranberry juice (Don't be a HAL—splurge and get the
   100 percent fruit juice instead of that artificial cranberry
   cocktail juice crap)
1 part pineapple juice
Seltzer

Start with a medium glass filled with ice, add Cognac, and follow it with the cranberry and then the pineapple juice, and you'll end up with pretty layers. Top with seltzer and frustration.

A gentleman always opens a door, but HAL is no gentleman. Although apologetic, he won't open the door for Dave. Dave gets his revenge by giving HAL a lobotomy. There might be a lesson to be learned here.

THE ADVENTURES OF BUCKAROO BANZAI ACROSS THE 8TH DIMENSION

Blue Blazer

The original Blue Blazer, developed in the late 1800s, involved setting scotch on fire and pouring the flaming blue liquid back and forth between two mugs. Don't do it. That's why I made something else that wouldn't put your life in jeopardy. Or cause a lawsuit, like my Flaming Moe cocktail.

1 part vodka
1/4 part blue curaçao
Ginger beer

Pour the vodka and curaçao into a medium glass filled with ice. Top with ginger beer.

Oscillator Overthruster

Drink until you are as insane as John Lithgow, arrive in the eighth dimension, or both. You'll need a blender or food processor for this one.

Makes 2 drinks.

3 scoops chocolate ice cream
1/2 part Baileys Irish Cream
1/2 part Kahlúa
3 scoops vanilla ice cream
1/2 part Stoli Razberi
1/2 part marshmallow vodka (you should have a ton left over
    from that *Ghostbusters* drink on page 105)
1/8 part Chambord for each drink (not necessary, but beautiful)

Put the chocolate ice cream, Baileys, and Kahlúa in a blender. Blend and oscillate, on overthrust speed, and divide the contents between two large glasses. Rinse out the blender.

Put the vanilla ice cream, Stoli, and marshmallow vodka in the blender. Blend and oscillate, on overthrust speed, and divide the contents over the chocolate mixture in the two large glasses. Pour Chambord over the top of each drink.

HEIDEL HINT

Hydration Protocol. Please, for the love of god, have a glass of water between each drink. Your friends, your bartender, and your future self will thank you. It not only helps to pace your alcohol consumption, but keeps you hydrated and prevents the dreaded Hangover Bladder Beast of Traal.

AGENTS OF S.H.I.E.L.D.

The Tahiti Effect

ILLUSTRATION BY KATI DELANEY

Whether you've been killed off by a god of Norse myth or just had a bad day at the office, this variation on the Tahiti will take you to a magical place. Palm trees optional.

1 part Bacardí Limón rum
1 part pineapple juice
7Up
Cranberry juice

Pour the rum and pineapple juice into a medium glass filled with ice. Fill almost to the top with 7Up and follow up with a splash of cranberry juice. Murmur "Please let me die" over and over while preparing.

Of Babes and Beasts:
An Ode to Ripley

BY CHLOÉ SEHR

Oh, Ripley, you live in a late-'70s early-'80s world about which the rest of us retain only a faint memory. You're rocking the white-lady perm, like so many of our moms back then, the one they would put up on the sides and back with plastic combs before they poured Mocha Mix in their morning coffee and lit up a cigarette at the breakfast table. Yes, smoking at the breakfast table, just like you and your semifearless crew in *Alien*, served with a side of good old-fashioned sexist banter. It's all so comforting. I can smell the Sizzlean now.

But they did you wrong, Ripley. No one remembered the most important piece of showbiz advice of them all, "Never work with animals or children" (often attributed to W. C. Fields).

So first, let's talk about the cat in *Alien*. Everyone knows that people don't kill people, aliens kill people who are looking for lost space cats. There are lots of rules to follow about how not to get murdered in a horror movie. For example: *Don't go anywhere alone!* But apparently, the sci-fi/horror hybrid makes spaceship personnel think that nothing bad can happen wandering around alone if one is engaged in the noble pursuit of finding the crew's pet kitty-cat. Those people are wrong. Sorry, Ripley. Brett and everyone else are dead and you must now go home alone, trapped in a box with the cat, taking the world's longest space nap.

Speaking of sequels, I think we can all agree that the only thing worse than a cat in space is a child in space, à la *Aliens*. Forget Newt's ear-bleeding scream for a moment. Forget that. Please. I'm trying so hard to forget that. What I want to talk about is that, yet again, the bad kid in the class is getting everyone in trouble on the field trip. Newt, when Ripley is trying to save you, please do not fall down an industrial fan (screaming, again!). Also, when she tries to find you with five minutes left until the whole goddamned place explodes, is that a good time to lose the very nice watch she gave you? Is that how you treat your things?

Ripley, I'm here for you. I know it's hard to be a badass when encumbered by ginger cats and grubby children. Here's my advice, for the alternate-universe version of both *Alien* and *Aliens*: leave them all behind. Kick alien ass, get on the spaceship, light up a smoke, and pour yourself a nice stiff drink (like the Chestburster) while you fly away, watching it all burn. You deserve it.

ALIEN

Chestburster

Here's a drink that you'll really feel in your chest. Is that burn you're feeling from all the peaty scotch? Or is that a baby alien ready to burst out of your gullet? After your fourth one, you'll beg your friends to kill you.

1 part the Peat Monster, Talisker, or other smoky/peaty scotch from the Islay region of Scotland
1/4 part ginger beer
Splash of lime juice

Pour all the ingredients into a small glass filled with ice. Stir.

In the immortal words of Bill Paxton's character, Private Hudson: "GAME OVER, MAN. Game over!"

Face Chugger
ILLUSTRATION BY TERESA GALUS

They mostly drink at night. Mostly.

1/2 part pilsner-style beer
1/2 part 7Up or other lemon-lime soda

Pour the ingredients into a large glass. Include a shot of your favorite booze on the side.

In space, no one can hear you scream. The reason: because you have a freakin' face hugger wrapped around your skull laying eggs down your throat. Not cool, man. So not cool.

BACK TO THE FUTURE

Flux Incapacitator

Great Scott! This cocktail makes drinking possible. Face your density.

1.21 gigawatts (1 part) white lightning, also known as moonshine Pepsi Free, Tab, or the modern equivalent diet cola

Pour the moonshine into a medium glass filled with ice and top with diet cola.

We are all time travelers. The problem is we can only move forward in time. However, with enough of this drink, it will appear as if you got there faster, and with a little less of your past intact. Enjoy responsibly . . . on a barstool, not in a DeLorean going eighty-eight miles an hour.

Doc B's Wake-up Juice

The following is based on my own personal remedy, invented when I had to work a brunch shift after staying out until 4 a.m. the night before.

1 part 100 percent agave tequila
1 part Bloody Mary mix
Splash each of lemon and lime juices
2 dashes bitters
2 dashes hot sauce (I prefer Cholula)

Pour all the ingredients into a large glass filled with ice. Shake, then strain into a small glass. Imagine a small atomic cloud appearing over the concoction. Drink all at once and revive.

If this is for a passed-out friend, you will need a clothespin and a funnel.

HEIDEL HINT

Remember when you are enjoying your bottomless mimosas and Bloody Marys that your server has probably had less sleep than you and might be more hungover than you. Be kind. Brunch is like a Grecian Hades for the serving class. Tip generously.

BABYLON 5

Babylon French 75

After four attempts at crafting this spin on the classic French 75 (one of them vanished completely), this fifth variant will help everyone get along.

1 part gin
1/4 part St-Germain
Splash of lemon juice
1/4 part Champagne or other sparkling wine

Pour the gin, St-Germain, and lemon juice into a large glass full of ice. Stir, then strain into a fancy glass and float the Champagne on top.

Sooner or later everyone comes for a Babylon French 75. Of course, since the French 75 is named after a gun, maybe not everyone will get along.

BATMAN

Bat Sidecar

Will Batman find all the ingredients? Will he make the cocktail in time? Can you dance the Batusi? Tune in next week!

2 parts bat Cognac
1 part bat triple sec
Splash of bat lemon juice

Pour all the ingredients into a large bat glass full of ice. Stir, then strain into a small bat glass.

Drink in your bat cave while working on your bat cycle.*
*Do not consume in front of your Batmobile's flame port.

HEIDEL HINT

Food Directive. I cannot stress this enough: *EAT* before you drink. Do I really have to tell you food will slow down the absorption rate of the alcohol you consume? That's science! When you drink on an empty stomach you will get sick and then cry about that lost cat you saw on a flyer.

BATTLESTAR GALACTICA

Starbuck

ILLUSTRATION BY ED REYNOLDS

There are those who believe
That drinks here began out there, far across the universe . . .

This tough yet beautiful drink embodies the soul of Starbuck.
SO DRINK WE ALL!

1 part bourbon
Rose lemonade

Fill a medium glass with lovingly crafted ice, add the tough bourbon of your choice, and then softly pour the rose lemonade to the top. Take a sip and you'll hear nothing but the rain.

BEETLEJUICE

Afterlife

ILLUSTRATION BY ELIZABETH DAGGAR

Dear Diary,
I am utterly alone. By the time you read this, I will be drunk, having ~~drank~~ imbibed at the Winter River Tavern.

1 part gin
1/4 part Aperol
2 parts ginger beer
Splash of lemon juice

Pour all the ingredients into a medium glass full of ice, give a stir, and enjoy.

The afterlife, much like life, involves a lot of bureaucracy. Take a ticket, wait a millennium, and make sure to fill out the proper forms in triplicate before crafting this drink.

BIG TROUBLE
IN LITTLE CHINA

Pork Chop Express

ILLUSTRATION BY ED REYNOLDS

*You know what ol' Andy Heidel says at a time like this? It's all in the
reflexes and not for nothin', we're not alone in the universe. When someone
wants to settle their tab and asks for a buyback, you know what I tell 'em?
A buyback is an honor, not a privilege.*

1 part Jägermeister
1 can of your favorite energy drink

Shoot the Jäger and chug your favorite energy
drink.

This will keep you truckin' all night long.

Pillars of Heaven

When the son of a bitch must pay, this is your drink. Especially when you bring a knife to a gunfight.

1 part vodka
1/2 part raspberry vodka
1/2 part peach schnapps

Pour all the ingredients into a small glass filled with ice. Stir.

BILL AND TED'S EXCELLENT ADVENTURE

Wyld Stallyns

This twist on the classic Italian Stallion is guaranteed to turn any bogus journey into an excellent adventure. You may pass your history final after drinking it, but probably not a breathalyzer.

1/2 part Frangelico
1/2 part amaretto
1/4 part absinthe

Pour all the ingredients into a small glass filled with ice. Stir.

Phone booth, police box . . . both will get you through time, but one is much cozier.

BLADE RUNNER

Blade Rummer

ILLUSTRATION BY ELIZABETH DAGGAR

I've drunk things you people wouldn't believe. Whiskey and cough syrup on fire off the shoulder of I-95. I quaffed a glittering gin and tonic in the black light near Hauser's Gate. All those cocktails will be lost in time, like tears . . . in . . . my brain. Time to cry.

1 part spiced rum
1/4 part Chambord
1 part orange juice
1 part pineapple juice
Splash of lime juice

Pour all the ingredients into a medium glass filled with ice. Stir, and dream of electric sheep.

Rum runners, unlike Blade Runners (who chase down Replicants), transported rum from the Caribbean to Florida during the Prohibition era. Like most drinks, the Rum Runner was created by a bar that had an abundance of its main ingredients—in this case, rum and banana liqueur. I, being a sane man and not a masochistic cocktail guide writer, didn't include banana liqueur in this drink. Also, Chloé hates bananas.

BRAZIL

Zipline Hero

Fresh mint
1/4 part lime juice
1 teaspoon sugar
1 part cachaça or white rum

In a small glass, muddle the mint, lime juice, and sugar. Fill the glass with ice, add the cachaça, and stir.

Tuttle is nowhere to be found, your ductwork has gone on the fritz, your apartment is at an unbearable temperature. Who do you call?

BUCK ROGERS IN THE 25TH CENTURY

Gin Buck Rogers

*The year is 1986 and NASA drinks the last of America's deep space shots.
In a freak mixology accident, Ranger 3 and its pilot, Captain William "Buck"
Rogers, are blown out of their drinking establishment into an orbit that
brain-freezes his life-support systems and returns Buck Rogers to the bar
five hundred years later.*

1 part gin
Ginger beer

Pour the gin into a medium glass full of ice, top up with ginger
beer, and garnish with a lime wedge.

It sucks being a fish out of water centuries in the future. Fortunately, there's a drink to help you get over the fact that everyone you ever knew and loved is dead.

A buck is any drink that contains ginger ale or ginger beer.

Bottoms Up Buffy

BY SARAH SHANOK

Just like some of the baddies our beloved Buffy and her loyal gang of Scoobies have battled, this slayer cocktail is two-faced—or three-faced, in the case of the Ghora demon—and blood red in color, because when it comes to the essence of the Buffyverse, there always has to be blood. As virile vampire Spike explained, "Blood is life, lack-brain. Why do you think we eat it? It's what keeps you going. Makes you warm. Makes you hard. Makes you other than dead."

So blood it must be for a Buffy beverage! But sangria isn't strong enough to pack an appropriate punch, and a Bloody Mary is too brunchy for a night-crawler cocktail, so The Gift is the perfect present to get you geared up for a routine evening of destroying demons, vanquishing vamps, or joining in on a game of kitten poker.

BUFFY THE VAMPIRE SLAYER

The Gift

ILLUSTRATION BY KATI DELANEY

The Gift is a cocktail that keeps on giving. When the end of the world comes, take this double-fisted shot before making the ultimate sacrifice.

1 part orange juice
3/4 part lime juice
1/2 part Pom pomegranate juice
3 dashes hot sauce or chili powder
1 part mezcal (Oaxacan preferred)

Pour all the ingredients except for the mezcal into a large glass. Shake or stir, then pour into a shot glass. Serve side by side with the shot of mezcal.

Hush

When blood is just the backstory to an episode, the cocktail gets a little more creative and shows its other face—just like the villains of "Hush," the ghoulish Gentlemen with metal teeth who inspire nightmares!

Hush the drink is an icy, frothy throwback to the days when everyone dressed to the nines and the drinks took time and effort to craft. When the Gentlemen come calling, this is the cocktail that will lift you off the ground and take your breath away.

2 parts Hendrick's gin
1/2 part heavy cream
1/2 part lemon juice
1/2 part lime juice
3/4 part simple syrup
3 dashes orange flower water or orange bitters
1 fresh egg white
Club soda
1 strawberry

Add all the ingredients except the club soda and strawberry to a shaker and shake vigorously without ice, or, if you don't have a shaker, whisk in a bowl. Open the shaker, fill with ice, and shake again or add ice to your bowl and whisk some more. Strain into a fancy glass. Pour a little bit of club soda back and forth between the empty halves of the shaker to pick up any residual egg white, then pour into the glass. (This will make for a frothier head.) Garnish with a thin slice of strawberry to resemble the hearts the Gentlemen carved from their victims.

HEIDEL HINT

Abort Mission. There is always a good chance you are on the verge of having too much to drink, and that you are about to make bad decisions. This is the last chance your cognitive brain has to make a good choice before the next drink, after which you might throw everything to the wind (or throw everything up). Take this opportunity to turn to your friend or bartender and ask for a cab home before your lizard brain takes charge. You don't want your lizard brain in charge!

CLOSE ENCOUNTERS OF THE THIRD KIND

Close Encounters of the Third Lime
ILLUSTRATION BY ELIZABETH DAGGAR

Here's one that will put a second-degree burn on half your face (or all your face, if you're doing it right). It's perfect for your next trip to Devil's Tower and points beyond. This drink means something.

1 part Tanteo jalapeño tequila
Pink grapefruit juice

Pour the tequila into a medium glass full of ice, top with grapefruit juice, and garnish with a lime slice.

Serve with a side of mashed potatoes.

Hum: G, A, F, (octave lower) F, C while you put together the ingredients.

CONAN THE BARBARIAN

Cognac the Barbarian
ILLUSTRATION BY ED REYNOLDS

What is best in life? Crush your lemons, see them driven into French cordials, and drink the libation of my creation.

1 part Cognac
1/2 part Grand Marnier
Splash of lemon juice

Pour all the ingredients into a large glass filled with ice. Stir, then strain into a fancy glass.

CONTACT

Cosmos-politan
ILLUSTRATION BY ED REYNOLDS

*We all need a Cracker Jack compass to help us find our
way back to Matthew McConaughey, don't we?*

1 part lemon vodka
1/4 part violet liqueur
1/4 part Chambord
1/4 part triple sec

Pour all the ingredients into a large glass filled with ice. Stir,
then strain into a fancy glass.

*Billyons upon billyons of years ago in this vast cosmic soup we know as the
universe, I created this drink. True story.*

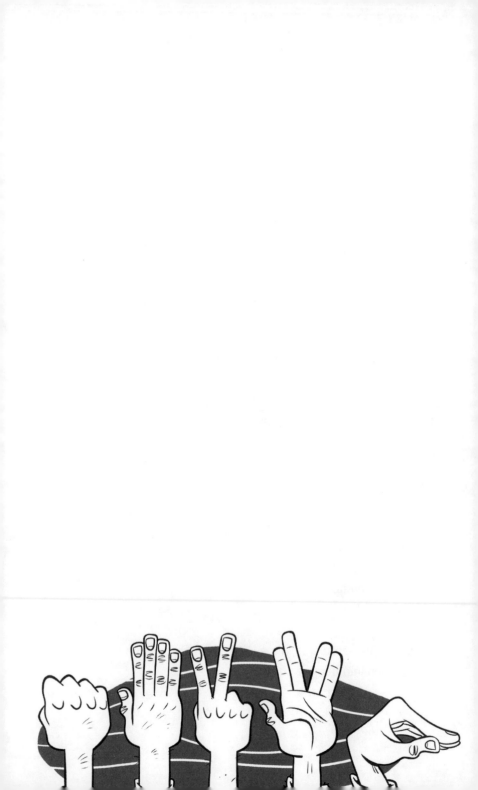

DISTRICT 9

District Lime

ILLUSTRATION BY ED REYNOLDS

Infected with alien DNA? No problem. This drink will get you back to the mothership.

1 part tequila
1/2 part cranberry juice
1/4 part lime juice

Pour all the ingredients into a large glass filled with ice. Shake, then pour into a medium glass.

ANDERS ANECDOTE

TRUMPET CASE

High school sucked, especially band. One day in band I dropped a quarter. The trumpeter sitting in front of me took it and wouldn't give it back. He even called me a "cheap Jew," which didn't make sense because I was asking for my own property back and I was Lutheran. So, when the conductor approached the podium and we all stood up, I pulled the first trumpet's chair back a few inches. When he went to sit, he fell to the floor. That was awesome. However, after class he threw me up against the lockers and threatened me. That was the opposite of awesome. I dropped out of band the following week and converted my trumpet case into a portable bar. Growing up, gin and tonic was my drink of choice, so I stocked my trumpet case with a 1 1/2-liter bottle of Gordon's gin, limes, and two bottles of tonic water and smuggled it into every high school party.

DOCTOR HORRIBLE'S SING-ALONG BLOG

Felicia Laundry Day
ILLUSTRATION BY KATI DELANEY

All you need is this cocktail, some quarters, and your freeze ray. Then, you and Felicia can make time stand still.

1 part the Bitter Truth violet liqueur
1 part Bombay Sapphire gin
1/4 part lemon juice

Pour all the ingredients into a large glass filled with ice. Stir, then strain into a fancy glass and garnish with a lemon peel. Drink it and feel those feelings you don't dare to feel.

Neil Patrick Hendrick's

First, work on your maniacal laugh. It's very important for this cocktail. Second, put on some gloves and don some goggles and an apron or lab coat. Third, tell Johnny Snow to go to hell.

1 part Hendrick's gin
1/2 part St-Germain
1 part pink grapefruit juice

Pour all the ingredients into a large glass filled with ice. Stir, then strain into a fancy glass.

This cocktail will impress Bad Horse and get you into the Evil League of Evil.

If it weren't for the Writers Guild strike of 2007–08 we never would have been treated to this amazing saga created out of boredom by out-of-work writers and actors. Go, unions!

Why We Built a TARDIS in Brooklyn
BY DOC WASABASSCO

It all happened because the author of this book—my oldest friend—decided to open a bar and, as old and good friends are wont to do for each other, I came on board to assist his vision and help create his space. It was to be a bar, a music venue, a place for the gathering of good, like-minded folks and kindred spirits—my friends, nerdy and true.

Low on capital but high on enthusiasm, we did much of the construction ourselves. Slowly, the bar and back bar, stage, and seating areas began to come together. An aesthetic had been chosen and we headed in that direction, but our labor of love was missing that iconic element, that hook, that draw, that "thing" that would make this venue stand out in the crowded sea of New York taverns and gathering places. A lifetime of big-city socializing had taught me that all of the most successful bars had a "thing": something to trigger the minds of any group of friends standing on a street corner arguing about where to go next—arguments that seldom include mention of ambience, but most likely include reference to iconic distinguishing features.

"I know," one drinker will say, "let's go to that place with that thing."

One day I saw it. A vision appeared before me while staring at the framed-out and yet-to-be-completed walls of the venue's central washroom. The framework itself sketched out the shape. I would build us a TARDIS . . . and . . . it would be bigger on the inside.

Inspired by my girlfriend's lifelong love of a British science fiction program (which had not yet reached the heights of popularity it was about to enjoy Stateside), and with my friend's enthusiastic support, I began to transform the external walls of the loo into a replica of the universe's most beloved conduit through Time And Relative Dimension In Space.

When the doors to my friend's venue, The Way Station, opened, the TARDIS was waiting. I will forever remember those early weeks of foot traffic, when an unsuspecting nerd strolling past the venue caught sight of her. The double take, the disbelief, stepping into the bar in shock, at a loss for words, ever so slowly walking over to touch the door to make sure she was real. Then staying for a drink.

Here we are, years later. The Way Station and the TARDIS have become, as intended, a gathering place and catalyst for the improvement of a multitude of lives, expansion of friendships, and initiation of numerous relationships. There have been business ventures, celebrity sightings, marriages, and the births of children, all sparked by the blue box in the corner—and, yes, the creation, preparation, selling, and imbibing of countless cocktails . . . contained within the pages of this book, and themed to the tastes of the geeky and nerdy: our kindred spirits.

DOCTOR WHO

Sonic Screwdrivers

The Doctor's most important tool, after his compassion and cleverness, is his sonic screwdriver. It's a scientific magic wand that is capable of altering or examining all kinds of things (as long as it's not made of wood, or dead-locked . . . why is it always deadlocked?). Luckily, there's already a popular cocktail called the Screwdriver, so now all we have to do is make it sonic.

Say, "That's Fantastic" when you try the 9th Doctor

1/4 part Pimm's (Why Pimm's, you ask? Because it is so damn British.)
1 part lemon vodka
Orange juice

Pour the Pimm's into a medium glass, add ice and the vodka, then top with orange juice.

Allons-y with the 10th Doctor

1/4 part blue curaçao
1 part lemon vodka
Orange juice

Pour the curaçao into a medium glass, add ice, and gently add the vodka, then top with orange juice. The effect should leave you with a colored "gem" at the bottom of the glass, reminiscent of the Doctor's sonic screwdriver's glowing tip. Serve as is, but you might want to stir before drinking.

Cocktails are cool with the 11th Doctor

1/4 part melon liqueur
1 part lemon vodka
Orange juice

Pour the melon liqueur into a medium glass, add ice, and gently add the vodka, then top with orange juice. The effect should leave you with a colored "gem" at the bottom of the glass, reminiscent of the Doctor's sonic screwdriver's glowing tip. Serve as is, but you might want to stir before drinking.

Discover spoilers with River's Red Setting

1/4 part grenadine
1 part lemon vodka
Orange juice

Pour the grenadine into a medium glass, add ice, and gently add the vodka, then top with orange juice. The effect should leave you with a colored "gem" at the bottom of the glass, reminiscent of River's sonic screwdriver's glowing tip. Serve as is, but you might want to stir before drinking.

I've been asked why we don't have a cocktail for every doctor at The Way Station. There are three truths: (1) there is only so much room on a cocktail menu; (2) having too many choices leads to slow decision making, and (c) it isn't always so easy to invent a drink to match a character. So for now, I present . . .

4th Doctor

You never forget your first Doctor. For me, it was Tom Baker. If you get this one right, it will be reminiscent of his trademark scarf.

1/4 part grenadine
2 parts pineapple juice
1 part dark rum

Pour the grenadine into a tall straight glass, then fill with ice. Add the pineapple juice and gently top with the dark rum.

Ironically, the fourth doctor hated celery, which brings us to . . .

5th Doctor

1 part London dry gin
Splash of celery bitters
1/4 part St-Germain
Soda water
Tonic water

Pour the gin, bitters, and St-Germain into a medium glass filled with ice. Top with half soda and half tonic.

12th Doctor

Why scotch? Because Capaldi is Scottish. Do you know how hard it is to make a cocktail out of a spirit that is already inherently perfect? It's pretty damn hard. That's why there are only five of them in this book.

1/2 part Dewar's scotch (or any other blended scotch)
1/2 part amaretto

Splash of Angostura bitters
Ginger ale

Pour the scotch, amaretto, and bitters into a medium glass filled with ice. Top with ginger ale.

Captain Jack

Everyone's favorite immortal interplanetary bisexual. This drink just might make you go all ways.

1/2 part Captain Morgan spiced rum
1/2 part Jack Daniel's whiskey
Cola

Pour the rum and whiskey into a large glass full of ice. Top with cola and garnish with a maraschino cherry.

Sexy, charming, and always up for a good time with anything or anyone.

Dark and Stormageddon

Ginger beer
1 part the Kraken dark rum

Fill a big glass with ice, fill almost to the top with ginger beer, then pour the rum on top. Garnish with a lime wedge.

Dalek Frolic

In-tox-icate!

1 part gin
1/4 part peach schnapps
1/4 part blue curaçao

Pour all the ingredients into a small glass filled with ice. Stir with a tiny plunger.

HEIDEL HINT

Unattended Proxy. Going out for a smoke or to use the TARDIS? (At The Way Station the lavatory is located inside the TARDIS.) Leave a coaster or a napkin on your drink and ask someone to keep an eye on it. This prevents your unattended cocktail from being cleared, or a Zombie Patron wandering off with your drink.

DUNE

Beer Is the Mind Killer
ILLUSTRATION BY TERESA GALUS

I must not beer. Beer is the mind killer. Beer is the little death that brings total obliteration. I will face my beer. I will permit it to pass over me and through me and when it has gone past I will turn to the inner eye to see its path. When the beer is gone there will be nothing. Only I will remain.

Kölsch, Jever, or pilsner beer
1/4 part Chambord

Fill a big glass almost to the top with beer. Add the Chambord.

The Spice must flow . . . down your throat.

ESCAPE FROM NEW YORK

Snake Blitzkin

Nobody is better at playing Kurt Russell than Kurt Russell.

1/2 part apple brandy
1/4 part Fireball Cinnamon Whisky
1/4 part sweet vermouth

Put on your eye patch. Pour all the ingredients into a large glass filled with ice. Stir, then strain into a fancy glass.

In the future, we still have cassette tapes with important data on them and steam-powered taxis on an island-turned-jail. Kurt's got this.

Biggest Rookie Mistakes People Make in a Bar Or in a Horror Film

Forgetting your credit card at the bar.

Separating from your group to explore alone.

Drinking multiple shots in a short amount of time.

Setting your weapon down and turning your back on it.

Not making it to the bathroom or outside if you feel sick to your stomach.

Not helping your drunk friend.

Taking the wrong coat.

Leaving your property unattended.

Reading aloud anything from some mysterious ancient text.

Reading to yourself a mysterious text from your ex.

Entering the woods at night.

Asking for a buyback.

Not having identification.

Tripping.

Not tipping.

Not leaving as soon as spooky shit starts going down.

Not leaving when you get sick.

Ordering a complicated drink not on the menu.

Having sex in the bathroom.
Hitting on the bartender.
Asking for a buyback.
Investigating a strange noise.
Begging for your life instead of defending it.
Asking for a buyback.

THE EVIL DEAD

Negroni-nomicon

ILLUSTRATION BY TERESA GALUS

The evil cocktail of the dead.

Perfect to drink while you read out loud in Latin from your favorite tome bound in human flesh. Don't speak Latin? You will after a few of these babies.

1 part gin
1/4 part Campari
1/4 part sweet vermouth
Tonic water

Pour the gin, Campari, and vermouth into a medium glass filled with ice. Top with tonic water and garnish with a lemon wedge.

Based on the classic Negroni but twice as sinister. Enjoy while reading A Farewell to Arms.

The Chin

Robert Mitchum, Kirk Douglas, and Cary Grant were all leading men who led with their chins, but none compares to Bruce Campbell. Like a Love-craftian monster, his chin defies description and commands both fear and respect simultaneously.

1/2 part bourbon
1/2 part rye
1/4 part red Lillet
1/8 part triple sec

Pour all the ingredients into a large glass filled with ice. Stir, then strain into a fancy glass. Garnish with a boomstick.

FANTASTIC FOUR

Fantastic Pour

All right. I give up. I can't invent this drink. We came up with a great name for it, but just like no one can seem to make a decent movie about this amazing comic, I can't make this cocktail. All I've got is . . .

Frozen whiskey stones
A pack of gum
A clear glass

Fill it with gasoline and set it on fire.

Enjoy!

FARSCAPE

Wormhole
ILLUSTRATION BY ED REYNOLDS

My name is Andy Heidel, a bartender. A boozy wave hit and I got a shot called the wormhole. Now I am lost in some distant part of Brooklyn, in a bar, a living bar full of strange nerds and geeks. Help me. Listen, please. Is there anybody out there who can hear me? I'm being hunted by an insane thirst. Doing everything I can. I'm just looking for a taxi home.

1 part Absolut Citron
1/4 part violet liqueur
1/4 part orange juice

Pour all the ingredients into a large glass filled with ice. Shake, then strain into a shot glass or two.

Aeryn Sunrise

This is my twist on a Tequila Sunrise but made with mezcal, because, like mezcal, Aeryn is smokin'.

1 part mezcal
1 part orange juice
1/4 part grenadine

Pour all ingredients into a small glass filled with ice.

ANDERS ANECDOTE

THE FIRST DRINK I EVER MADE

When I was sixteen, my mom went away for the weekend and I raided the liquor cabinet. It was a Saturday night and I was listening to WLIR radio, the only station around that played nothing but New Wave. Believing I was being sneaky, I poured a minute amount of liquor from various bottles: gin, whiskey, vodka, amaretto, grappa, vermouth, and some things I couldn't pronounce, until I had a full glass of booze and none of the bottles looked like they had ever been touched. It tasted terrible but it got me drunk, which was the intention, but then it got me violently ill, which was not. I spent the next day in bed with a splitting headache and a queasy stomach. I learned a very important lesson: don't ever do that again. The more important lesson . . . learn how to make a decent drink.

THE FIFTH ELEMENT

Divinian

ILLUSTRATION BY ELIZABETH DAGGAR

A cocktail put together as divinely as Leeloo herself.

1 part gin (preferably Comb 9)
1 teaspoon St-Germain or other elderflower liqueur
1 teaspoon olive brine (from your jar of queen stuffed olives)
1 teaspoon lime juice

Pour all the ingredients into a large glass filled with ice. Stir, then strain into a fancy glass.

This combination of salty, sweet, sour, and bitter creates the fifth taste, known as umami. Behold, the Divinian. Make it with love.

I've made three unforgettable drinks in my lifetime. This, the Awesome Mixed Drink, and Barrelhound of the Baskervilles (originally the '87 Grant made with twenty-one-year-old Glenfiddich). When this cocktail is made properly, it is really good. When it's made perfectly, it is divine.

FIREFLY

Captain Tight Pants

For those times when you aim to misbehave, I concocted this to increase your swagger and charming smile. I was going to rewrite the lyrics to the opening song, but (1) they don't reckon well with wordplay and (b) I can't liken my skills as a lyricist to those of Joss Whedon. I might be kissing some galactic ass here. Just sayin', but we're talking about a man who brought us some of the best sf/f musical scores of all time.

Captain Lawrence Clearwater Kölsch or pilsner-style beer
1/4 part Firefly Apple Pie moonshine

Fill a big glass almost to the top with the beer. Add the moonshine.

Shiny

1/4 part Grand Marnier
Champagne

Pour the Grand Marnier into a fancy glass, then top with Champagne.

Leaf on the Wind

There will be times in your life when you are in the groove, avoiding obstacles while achieving your goal. You might be tempted to utter the phrase, "I'm a leaf on the wind," but remember: as soon as you land . . . BAM, right in the chest.

Dry vermouth
1 part chilled sparkling wine
1 part chilled lemon-lime soda
1/4 part Chambord

First, give a fancy glass a dry vermouth wash. (A wash is when you are stabbed through the chest, just when you think everything is safe. A wash is also bartending jargon for rinsing the inside of a glass with a minute amount of spirits, then pouring out any excess.) Add the remaining ingredients.

This drink has a delicate touch with devastating consequences.

Mudder's Milk

1/4 part Stoli Vanil vodka
1/4 part Kahlúa
Milk stout or your favorite dark beer

Pour the Stoli and Kahlúa into a big glass, then top with milk stout. Afterward, do something of dubious merit to inspire a folk song.

Serenitea

In all good sci-fi, the ship itself is a character. The captain and crew love and bleed for her.

Fresh mint
1 part Firefly Sweet Tea vodka
lemon-lime soda

Tear the mint into tiny pieces, then put it in the bottom of a medium glass full of ice. This helps express the oils and thwart the Reavers. Add the vodka and top with lemon-lime soda. Garnish with a lemon wedge and a tiny plastic dinosaur.

FLASH GORDON

Green Flash Gordon

Just as Flash Gordon is classic sci-fi, the Green Flash is a classic cocktail.

1 part vodka
1/4 part peach schnapps
1/4 part blue curaçao
1/4 part melon liqueur
1/4 part amaretto
1/2 part orange juice
1/2 part lemon-lime soda

Pour all the ingredients into a large glass full of ice, adding the soda last and stirring gently.

FUTURAMA

Bender's Bender
ILLUSTRATION BY KATI DELANEY

No one is better at being drunk, self-centered, narcissistic, but totally endearing than Bender. Here's one only for those with an iron stomach. We can't promise that it won't leave a little rust on you, but it's perfect fuel for your comic belligerence.

1 bottle of bourbon
1 box of cigars

Not sure if this is a good idea . . . or a great idea.

GALAXY QUEST

Galaxy Quench
ILLUSTRATION BY TERESA GALUS

Always drink up. Never surrender!

1/2 part Stoli Vanil vodka
1/2 part Stoli Ohranj vodka
1/4 part triple sec
Coconut water
Ginger beer

Pour the vodkas and triple sec into a medium glass filled with ice. Top with equal parts coconut water and ginger beer.

Grabthar's Hammered

By Grabthar's hammer, by the tongues of Barvan, you shall be unhinged.

1 part Malibu coconut rum
1/4 part peach schnapps
lemon-lime soda

Pour the rum and schnapps into a medium glass filled with ice.
Top with lemon-lime soda.

HEIDEL HINT

Shooting Gallery. We all get caught up in the moment and want to celebrate by doing shots. Be sure to pace your shots. The dopamine you experience makes you want to buy another round, but wait an hour or two between them. If you don't: LIZARD BRAIN!

GAME OF THRONES

George R. R. Martini
ILLUSTRATION BY KATI DELANEY

The best thing about Game of Thrones *is that all of your favorite characters get killed off. In similar fashion, you'll want to finish off several of these martinis in creative and violent ways. Be warned, like Martin's novels, this cocktail can take two to four years to create.*

2 parts gin
1/4 part dry vermouth

Let sit on the shelf for a year.

Add ice, stir, and contemplate.

Come back to it later.

Strain into a fancy glass.

Garnish with one olive stabbed through the heart with a lemon wedge.

The Blood of My Enemies

Grab a glass. Fill it with whiskey. Sit in your favorite chair and think of those you hate and how you will kill them, and of taking over the Seven Kingdoms.

GHOSTBUSTERS

Ecto Cooler

ILLUSTRATION BY ELIZABETH DAGGAR

Here's one (alcoholic) spirit you'd love to keep busting. Who you gonna call? (A cab to get you home, silly.)

1 part Old Overholt rye
1/4 part pickle juice
Ginger ale

Pour the rye and pickle juice into a medium glass filled with ice. Top with ginger ale and garnish with a six-hundred-pound Twinkie.

Drink in a haunted library and go bye-bye.

COMMERCIAL BREAK

ANDERS: *Are you troubled by strange feelings in the middle of the day?*

COREY: *Do you experience feelings of dread in your home or office?*

CHLOÉ: *Have you or any of your family ever drank bourbon, rye, or whiskey?*

ANDERS: *If the answer is yes, then don't wait another minute. Grab a taxi and visit the professionals.*

ANDERS, COREY, CHLOÉ: *The Way Station!*

ANDERS: *Our courteous and efficient staff is on call twelve hours a day to serve all your intoxication needs.*

ANDERS, COREY, CHLOÉ: *We're ready to serve you!*

Stay Puffed

When dogs and cats are living together, this martini of biblical proportions will keep you mallow.

Did you notice that Dana's shopping choices included marshmallows and eggs? What the hell was she going to make? A s'mores omelet? Believe it or not, that's the inspiration for this cocktail. And it's surprisingly good. Trust me here, I'm a professional.

1 part Pinnacle marshmallow vodka
1/4 part crème de cacao
1/4 part mezcal
1 egg white

Put all the ingredients in a shaker. Yes, I know I said at the beginning of the book that you didn't need to use a shaker. If you don't have a shaker, put all the ingredients in a bowl. Shake or whisk for 30 seconds. Add ice, then shake or whisk for 30 seconds more. This ensures the egg white becomes frothy and is integrated into the ingredients. Strain into a fancy glass.

When I shared this cocktail with my regulars, my favorite response was: "What did you do, Anders?"

Playlist by KBRI

"I'd Love to Change the World," Ten Years After

"(Don't Fear) The Reaper," Blue Oyster Cult

"Go Your Own Way," Fleetwood Mac

"Solsbury Hill," Peter Gabriel

"Jolene," Dolly Parton

"Ooh La La," Faces

"I Fought the Law," The Clash

"Fly by Night," Rush

"Meanwhile Back at the Ranch," Badfinger

"You're My Best Friend," Queen

"Walk on the Wild Side," Lou Reed

"On the Road to Find Out," Cat Stevens

"Blinded by the Light," Bruce Springsteen

"Crazy on You," Heart

"Jeepster," T. Rex

"Higher Ground," Stevie Wonder

"Fooling Yourself," Styx

"I've Seen All Good People," Yes

The Mix Tape

Once upon a time there was an archaic audio device called the cassette player, also known as a tape recorder. One would put a cassette into the contraption and the spooled magnetic tape would play music. These same tapes were also used to load programs onto early home computers.

I would stay up late listening to WLIR-FM, my Maxell tape engaged on pause/record, and as soon as my favorite New Wave song started, I would undo pause to record that song from a radio station fifty miles away. I had thirty of these WLIR mix tapes. This is important: there are two types of mix tapes. The first is the one you make for a friend, to introduce new songs or show off your knowledge of obscure bands. The second, and more important, is the one you make for someone you have an enormous crush on and want to impress by including songs that have been played on your dates, or that remind you of this person, or favorite songs that speak to your soul.

DJs like Larry the Duck, Malibu Sue, and Donna Donna were my heroes. When I was a kid, making a mix tape made me feel like I was the DJ, like I was the hero.

GUARDIANS
OF THE GALAXY

The Awesome Mixed Drink
ILLUSTRATION BY KATI DELANEY

Making a drink to stand up to this name is a tall order. Fortunately, I had this time-tested and true cocktail in my back pocket from the days when I was still making mix tapes.

1/4 part each of:

Captain Morgan rum
Maker's Mark Bourbon
Southern Comfort
Amaretto
Lime juice
Triple sec

Pour all the ingredients into a large glass filled with ice. Shake or stir, then strain into a fancy glass.

I Am Root

1 part Stoli Vanil vodka
1/2 part Root liqueur
1/4 part Kahlúa

Pour all the ingredients into a small glass filled with ice and grow back.

We Are Root

1/2 part Root liqueur
Alcoholic root beer

Pour the Root into a medium glass filled with ice and top with root beer.

HIGHLANDER

The Quickening

There can be only one . . . drink! Actually, what the hell . . . make it a double!

1 part blended scotch (I suggest Monkey Shoulder or
  Barrelhound)
1/4 part Bénédictine
1/4 violet liqueur
Splash of lime juice

Pour all the ingredients into a large glass filled with ice. Stir, then strain into a small glass.

ANDERS ANECDOTE

I'M A BOOK NERD

I moved a lot as a kid and didn't get to make or keep many friends. Books became the only constant in my life, and those imaginary worlds were so much more reliable than the reality of my new town or school. Incredibly, those books that I escaped into actually helped me make new friends, because other kids read them, too. Thank you to *The Chronicles of Narnia*, *The Hobbit*, and *Lord of the Rings*, battered and tattered, dog-eared and worn. You helped me make friends with Soren Rasmussen in the sixth grade, who then introduced me to my new holy grail of literature, *The Hitchhiker's Guide to the Galaxy*, which then helped me make even more friends.

. . . And the trail of books and friends continues to this day.

THE HITCHHIKER'S GUIDE TO THE GALAXY

Pan Galactic Gargle Blaster

ILLUSTRATION BY KATI DELANEY

Considered the most dangerous drink in the galaxy, the Pan Galactic Gargle Blaster (invented by Douglas Adams) contains some very exotic spirits not found on our planet. Below is my interpretation of the legendary cocktail using ingredients that can be found on Earth that will knock your socks off. If you are not wearing socks, I suggest you put some on before trying this truly omnipotent cocktail.

First of all, make sure you have your towel.

1/4 part each of:

Goldschläger
Fireball Cinnamon Whisky

Absinthe
Jägermeister
St-Germain
Lemon juice

Pour all the ingredients into a large glass filled with ice. Stir, then strain into a fancy glass and garnish with a lemon peel.

Drink, but very carefully.

TASTING NOTES BY ELVIS BOB RASPUTIN

Nose: It smells like Christmas but on the street, like the chilly air while peering through the glass at a window display.

Opening: Sweet, with a hint of darkness and some exotic spice that only Southeast Asians can truly identify.

Middle: Growing darkness . . . wait! That turned on me really fast; this is going somewhere I don't think I want to go. Aaaaaaaaahhh! Nooooo!

Finish: A little acidic. My mouth feels funky.

Follow-up: Something is punching my stomach from the inside. It might be my liver.

Recommendation: This might be my favorite drink of all time. Well, my favorite as long as I consume with weeks or months between drinks.

AUTHOR'S NOTE: I had to take dictation for his final thoughts: "Face numb, internal organs stopped fighting, can't see. Totally unaware of my nipples. I can't write."

THE HUNGER GAMES

The Thirsty Games (A Drinking Game)

Have your allies in order. You name an actor. Your next ally has to name a movie that actor died in. The next ally has to name a different actor in that film. Your next ally has to name a different movie that actor died in. This goes on till someone is stumped. Whoever cannot answer correctly has do a shot of Captain Morgan Cannon Blast spiced rum.

INDIANA JONES

Shirley Temple of Doom
ILLUSTRATION BY KATI DELANEY

The Shirley Temple is a classic drink for kids, so don't let Short Round see when you pour a little whiskey in yours. Your respect for this drink will go way up when you realize there's not a drop of Crystal Skull (vodka) in it!

1 part Old Overholt rye
Ginger ale
1/4 part grenadine or maraschino cherry juice

Pour the whiskey into a large glass filled with ice. Pour the ginger ale almost to the top, then add the grenadine. Garnish with a still-beating heart, a cherry, and a lemon wedge.

If Only You Spoke Mojitos

The line "If only you spoke Hovitos," delivered by Indiana Jones's archrival Belloq, always stuck with me. It states simply that knowledge is power.

3 mint leaves
1 teaspoon sugar
3/4 part lime juice
1 part silver rum
Club soda

In a large glass, muddle the mint, sugar, and lime juice. Add the rum, then fill the glass with ice. Stir, then pour into a medium glass and top with club soda.

Here's a Heidel Hint: *The most important knowledge regarding mojitos is that bartenders hate making them.*

The Holy Rail

The quest for the holy rail should never be taken lightly. Men have died in its pursuit.

1 part silver tequila
1 part vodka
1 part gin
1 part silver rum
1/2 part triple sec
Splash of lemon juice
Splash of cola

Pour all the ingredients into a large glass filled with ice. Stir, and—whatever you do—choose wisely and make sure to drink it from *the right cup*!

INVASION OF THE BODY SNATCHERS

Invasion of the Toddy Snatchers

If a body-snatched Donald Sutherland ever comes near, points at you, and lets out a horrifying shriek—stuff one of these in his face to shut him up quick.

1 part whiskey
Tea bag of choice (I recommend orange pekoe or Earl Grey)
Honey to taste
Juice of 1/2 lemon

Put all the ingredients in your favorite coffee mug. Add hot water. Let the tea steep for 3 to 5 minutes. Remove the tea bag, stir, and enjoy.

JURASSIC PARK

Jurassic Dark Daiquiri

The daiquiri, much like dinosaur DNA, has been abused and perverted far from its original incarnation. My take on the original daiquiri is beautiful in its simplicity. It won't bite.

1 part dark spiced rum such as the Kraken
1/4 part maraschino liqueur
1/4 part lime juice

Pour all the ingredients into a small glass filled with ice. Stir, then strain into a fancy glass.

LOST IN SPACE

Sauced in Space

This drink is danger, Will Robinson, danger.

1 part Cognac
1 part amaretto
1 part dark spiced rum
Splash of lemon juice

Pour all the ingredients into a large glass filled with ice. Stir, then strain into a fancy glass.

Enjoy with friends and—most important—family. Never share with Dr. Smith.

LORD OF THE RINGS

My Precious

ILLUSTRATION BY ED REYNOLDS

The next time you gather your Fellowship of the Drinking, beware this: the one, true (condensation) ring (those things will ruin the wood). My Precious will call to you. You'll do anything for it.

1 part Bombay Sapphire gin
1/4 part Amaro Meletti
1/4 part Grand Marnier
Splash of lemon juice

Pour all the ingredients into a large glass filled with ice. Stir, then strain into a fancy glass.

Side effects may include invisibility, madness, and the loss of a finger.

Gandalf the Greylock

2 parts Greylock gin
1/4 part St-Germain
1/4 part Chartreuse
1/4 part lemon juice

Pour all the ingredients into a large glass filled with ice. Stir, then strain into a fancy glass.

Gimli

1 part Brockmans gin
1/4 part triple sec
1/4 part lime juice

Pour all the ingredients into a medium glass filled with ice. Stir, enjoy.

Back in the day, a brockman, also known as a brook man, was the dude who had to find a fresh stream for the gin distillers in London because the Thames had gone as sour as Gimli.

THE MARTIAN

Marstini

Hey there, Space Pirate, this is perfect for when you're low on supplies and need to science the shit out of a drink.

1 part booze
1 part juice
Something bubbly

Pour booze and juice into a medium glass filled with ice. Top with that bubbly substance and garnish with a potato. Make sure to document the process.

MAD MAX

V8 Interceptor
ILLUSTRATION BY ED REYNOLDS

Max always has a cool car.
Max can't always hold on to his cool car.
Max usually crashes his cool car.
Don't be like Max. Take a taxi when you go to the Chunderdome on Furry
Road, you warrior.

1 part whiskey
Dash of hot sauce
2 dashes Worcestershire sauce
Stout beer
V8 vegetable juice

Pour the whiskey, hot sauce, and Worchestershireshieririre sauce into a large glass filled with ice. Top with equal parts beer and V8.

THE MATRIX

Blue Shot/Red Shot

ILLUSTRATION BY ELIZABETH DAGGAR

This is your last drink. After this, there is no turning around. You take the blue shot—the night ends, you wake up in your bed with a hangover, and you're late for work. You take the red shot—you stay in Wonderbar and I show you how fun a night of drinking can be.

Blue Shot

1 part silver rum
1/4 part blue curaçao
1/4 part pineapple juice

Pour all the ingredients into a large glass filled with ice. Stir, then strain into a shot glass.

Red Shot

1 part tequila
1/4 part grenadine
1/4 part orange juice

Pour all the ingredients into a large glass filled with ice. Stir,
then strain into a shot glass.

MEN IN BLACK

Neuralizer

Okay, champ, tiger, scout, slick, kid, sport, if you're gonna ride with me, you need one of these, based on the classic Mind Eraser.

1 part Kahlúa
1 part mezcal
Soda water

Pour the Kahlúa into a large glass full of ice, then pour in the mezcal and top with soda water. Suck it down with a straw.

There's a good chance you'll see some pretty alien things when under the influence of the Neuralizer. But don't worry, you won't remember any of them in the morning.

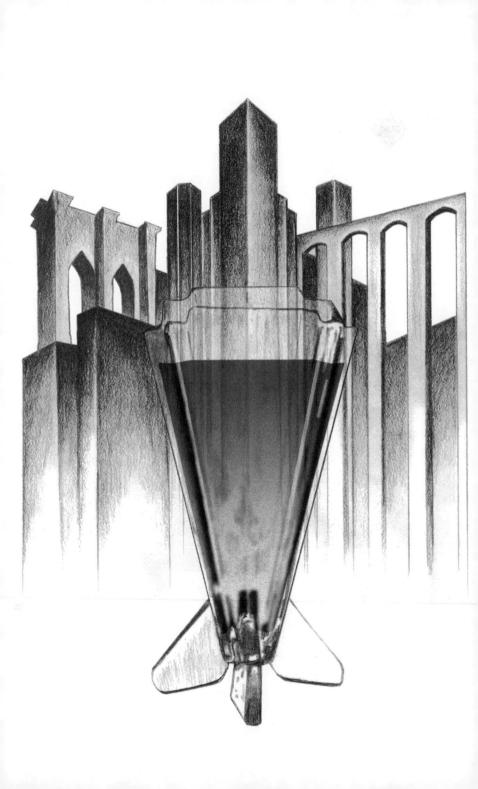

The Metropolis

ILLUSTRATION BY ELIZABETH DAGGAR

DIRECTED BY R ANDREW HEIDEL
PRODUCED BY THE WAY STATION
A BROOKLYN BAR PRODUCTION

The Mediator between the Patron and the liver must be the Bartender

1 part rye
1/4 part Aperol
1/4 part sweet vermouth
Dash of bitters
1/8 part Champagne

Pour the rye, Aperol, vermouth, and bitters into a large glass filled with ice. Shake or stir, then strain into a fancy glass. Float the Champagne on top.

HEIDEL HINT

Med Bay. Know your meds and how they interact with alcohol. Also alert your friends to any possible interactions. It will be the difference between a good time you remember or an unsafe blackout night you'll regret. Trust me, it's awkward having your friends or bartender fill in the blanks the following day.

MYSTERY SCIENCE THEATER 3000

Satellite of Love

ILLUSTRATION BY TERESA GALUS

In the not-too-distant past
Last Sunday A.D.
There was a guy named Anders
Not too different from you or me
He worked as a bartender every day
Just pushing cocktails, to pay his way
He did his job well with a gleeful face
But his bosses didn't like him so they fired him from that place!

1 part Stoli Ohranj vodka
1/2 part Chambord

1/2 part pineapple juice
Splash of lemon juice

Pour all the ingredients into a small glass filled with ice. Stir, then strain into two shot glasses.

FAVORITE UNDERRATED MOVIES

Dead Snow
Black Sheep
Big Trouble in Little China
The Wave
The Adventures of Buckaroo Banzai Across the 8th Dimension
Repo Man
Shadow of the Vampire
Kung Fury
Iron Sky

PIRATES OF THE CARIBBEAN

Release the Kraken
ILLUSTRATION BY KATI DELANEY

You too can drink like Captain Jack Sparrow when this beastie from deep within Davy Jones's liquor cabinet comes for your liver. Be forewarned: tangle with this tasty, tentacled treat at your own risk and that of your drinking crew. Savvy?

Ginger beer
1 part the Kraken dark spiced rum (you can use any dark rum, but it is far more fun to use Kraken rum because when you open the bottle you get to say, "Release the Kraken!")
Splash of lime juice

Fill a medium glass with ice and pour in the ginger beer to 1 inch from the top. Add the rum and lime juice. Garnish with a lime wedge and fear.

It's no curse when this drink pulls you under.

According to legend, the Kraken was hunted to extinction in order to produce this exotic rum. Oddly, it has been rumored that the elusive and eccentric distiller of Kraken Rum is named Seamus McKraken. Coincidence?

PLANET
OF THE APES

Damn Dirty Grapes

You'll want to get your filthy paws on this one! Drink carefully and try not to blow up Earth, you maniac!

2 parts Cîroc vodka (or any other vodka distilled from grapes, like Hangar 1)
1/4 part dry vermouth
1/4 part olive brine

Pour all the ingredients into a large glass filled with ice. Stir, then strain into a fancy glass. Garnish with a grape.

I was totally overthinking this cocktail and almost tried to make something with grappa, wine, and Champagne that would have led to the worst hangover of your life. You're welcome.

When Charlton Heston damns you all to hell, remember: he's a gun nut.

ANDERS ANECDOTE

HANGOVER HELPER

Sometimes it is not your fault that you have a hangover when all you drank last night was three draft beers. I discovered that when I drank draft at certain bars I would have a hangover the next day, while at others, drinking the same quantity, I wouldn't. The culprit? Dirty draft lines with a yeasty beasty. Think of a draft line as a long crazy straw that runs from a keg in a beer cooler in the basement twenty to fifty feet away all the way to the tap. Now imagine that you use the same straw every day without cleaning it. Bacteria and yeast build up in the line and taint the beer. In one instance a slug of yeast and bacteria poured out of the tap and into my friend's beer. He took a swig and that wad of grossness ended up in his mouth. Fortunately, he didn't swallow. That's why I clean my beer lines every two weeks and why you should avoid draft beers unless the bartender knows the last time the lines have been cleaned.

REPO MAN

Repo Manhattan
ILLUSTRATION BY ELIZABETH DAGGAR

Dead radioactive aliens in your car trunk? No problem. Deal with tense situations with this drink.

2 parts generic rye
1/2 part generic sweet vermouth
2 dashes generic bitters

Pour all the ingredients into a large glass filled with ice. Stir, then strain into a solo cup. Garnish with a generic cherry.

When you want to blame society for your actions, remember you're a white suburban punk, just like me.

RICK AND MORTY

Rick and Forty

ILLUSTRATION BY ELIZABETH DAGGAR

Rick: Uncle Morty, should you really be drinking and driving?
Morty: Rick, (burp) it's a spaceship, so technically, I'm not driving, but
actually flying.

At least one 40-ounce bottle of your favorite malt liquor. Take a
few swigs, then fill to the top with whiskey from your flask.

SHERLOCK HOLMES

7 Percent Solution

ILLUSTRATION BY ELIZABETH DAGGAR

Holmes famously utilized cocaine to stimulate his brain. While we can't condone the use of that illegal substance, we assure you this elemental drink will jolt your senses and allow you to see all the clues in life other people are missing.

Fun fact: In the early 1900s one could purchase cocaine legally in forms such as Coca-Cola or infant toothache remedy.

1/2 part absinthe
1/2 part Jägermeister
7Up

Pour the absinthe and Jägermeister into a medium glass filled with ice. Top up with 7Up.

This is the kind of drink Robert Downey Jr., Benedict Cumberbatch, and Jonny Lee Miller could all enjoy together.

Barrelhound of the Baskervilles

A sales rep dropped by the bar on a dark and stormy night. Suddenly, the lights went out. We were all engulfed in darkness. Moments later, the lights flicked back on. The sales rep was gone. In his place, a bottle of Barrelhound blended scotch, with a note: "If you ever want to see him alive again, create a cocktail strong enough to lift a curse."

1 part Barrelhound blended scotch
1/4 part Barrow's Intense Ginger or other ginger liqueur
1/4 part sweet vermouth
Two dashes of dandelion burdock bitters

Pour all the ingredients into a small glass filled with ice. Stir. The game is now afoot.

SNOWPIERCER

Train Wreck

"Did you know babies taste best?"

Years ago I wrote the Stroller Manifesto, which stated that children shouldn't be in bars. After seeing this movie, I have to add that they also don't belong in engine compartments.

1 cucumber slice (approximately 1/2 inch in width)
1 part gin
1 part pink grapefruit juice
1/4 part cranberry juice

Toss the cucumber in the bottom of a glass. Use a muddler, wooden spoon, or end of a baseball bat to mash it (three to six good mashings). Fill glass with ice, add the remaining ingredients, and shake (or stir if you don't have a shaker, though for this one drink, the shaker really comes in handy).

This movie, just like some of my cocktails, shouldn't work for a million reasons, but somehow it does.

Welcome to Barfleet Academy with Corey Lange

Welcome, Ensign. Before we step into the holodeck, go back in time, and experience a twenty-first-century bar, here is some advice that will aid you in your goal of having an intergalactic good time. Tipping was part of American culture . . . at least until the twenty-fourth century, when the New World Economy abolished the concept of monetary value.

While inconceivable now, even to Guinan, bartenders across twenty-first-century America earned at most minimum wage (approximately $7.50 per hour as of 2017, the equivalent value of a Tribble pelt in today's black-market economy). For a bartender skilled in multitasking, advanced psychology, and hospitality, that was a pittance considering their skill set, and would not cover the cost of archaic things such as rent and bills. So, why did they do this? Because of tipping.

Twenty-first-century bartenders relied on tips to make a living, so don't be a Ferengi during your visit. The Prime Directive stipulates that tipping 15 to 20 percent of your total bill is essential to bartenders' continued well-being, but if you really want to get a bartender's attention, tip 30 to 40 percent on your first drink, especially if it is as crowded as

Ten Forward on stardate 46379.1. Bartenders who do their job correctly will notice this and you will be VIP from this point on (VIP is a colloquial term for very important person, like Ambassador Spock), resulting in you receiving quicker service and better attention. Continue to follow this technique, and treat your bartender like the sentient being that they are, and you might receive the elusive "buyback" generally received after three or four drinks. (YOU MUST NEVER ASK FOR THIS.) If you receive the mysterious buyback, tip at least three dollars or up to half the cost of the drink.

The hardest thing for us in the New World Economy to understand about the twenty-first century is that back then, money worked. When twenty-first-century customers tipped, they subsidized bartenders' financial well-being and bartenders returned the favor by contributing to their enjoyment of the evening. That being said, not all bartenders are created equal (think Data and Lore), and if they aren't rewarding your good behavior, just tip the regular amount of 15 to 20 percent. No need to pay for service that you're not getting.

All that being said, enjoy this complimentary red shirt.

STAR TREK

Hair of the Worf

Years ago I woke up hungover and said to my roommate, "Doc, I need a hairy dog." "Hair of the dog," he corrected me. "As in hair of the dog that bit you." This means that a little bit of what hurt you can cure you. This is true for vaccines and hangovers. When you get bit by Worf, you need something a little more serious.

1 part whiskey
2 parts V8 vegetable juice, tomato juice, or Bloody Mary mix
2 splashes Sriracha hot sauce
2 splashes lemon juice

Pour all the ingredients into a medium glass filled with ice.

Warp Core Sex on the Breach
ILLUSTRATION BY ED REYNOLDS

While we saw very few sexual encounters on the Enterprise *(Data, I know you are fully functional, please step back), it is a little-known fact that the engineering staff engages in adrenaline-fueled orgies after preventing a warp core breach. With just enough vodka to keep Chekov dancing, this cocktail is sure to provide the fuel you need.*

1 part vodka
1/4 part peach schnapps
1/4 Barrow's Intense ginger liqueur
1/4 Chambord
1 part orange juice
1 part pineapple juice

Pour all the ingredients into a large glass filled with ice. Stir or shake. Garnish with a maraschino cherry.

Star Trek has always featured salacious smooching (see: Uhura's Kiss, page 177) as well as scantily clad ensigns and aliens. While carnal events have been insinuated, none was ever so overtly implied as in the episode "The Naked Now," in which Data was propositioned by a very intoxicated Tasha Yar. It was a memorable moment for the happy couple, and honestly something no television viewer ever needed to see.

Well Wheaton

1 part silver tequila
1 part vodka
1 part gin
1 part silver rum
1/2 part triple sec
Splash of lemon juice
Splash of cola

Pour all the ingredients into a large glass filled with ice. Stir or shake, then enjoy a nice long game of D&D with your friends.

Wil Wheaton has admirably escaped the whiny reputation of his Star Trek character Wesley Crusher. We toast Wil with this drink, named in his honor. Drink while reading one of his fantastic memoirs—required reading for all nerds.

Romulan Ale

Set your phasers to rum for this drink.

1 part silver rum
1/4 blue curaçao
Pineapple juice

Pour the rum and curaçao into a medium glass filled with ice. Top with pineapple juice.

He's Dead, Gin

BY ELIZA HECHT

Star Trek is, without question, one of the most iconic science-fiction series of all time. The holy trinity of Captain Kirk, Mister Spock, and Dr. McCoy was the heart of a franchise that still resonates with viewers today.

Kirk may have been the sexy one and Spock may have been the smart one, but McCoy was the human one. He was intelligent, competent, and likable.

Dr. McCoy didn't just have common sense; he made sure everyone else knew it too. The even-keeled doctor always spoke his mind, often in colorful, memorable ways. If Spock suggested something McCoy didn't agree with, the doctor was there with, "Are you out of your Vulcan mind?" If Kirk left before the end of a necessary physical, McCoy called after him with a sarcastic, "What am I, a doctor or a moon shuttle conductor?"

Whether the ill-fated redshirts were suffering from bacterial infections that made them horny or were being attacked by salt-sucking creatures disguised as beautiful women, McCoy treated every affliction. And then, when they met their unfortunate demise, Dr. McCoy pronounced them deceased with perhaps the series's most famous catchphrase: "He's dead, Jim."

Captain Kirk was probably a whiskey drinker. It's a sexy drink, fit for a man's man. And Spock undoubtedly preferred practical vodka, efficient and no frills. But McCoy? McCoy had dimension. Subtlety. Sophistication. McCoy definitely liked gin.

He's Dead, Gin

Dammit, Gin. I'm a bartender, not a doctor! How do you expect me to save lives with these ingredients?

Absinthe
1 part Death's Door gin (or London dry gin)
1/4 part amaretto

Rinse a fancy glass with absinthe. (A rinse is: adding a thimbleful of liquid to your glass first, swirling it around, and pouring out the excess.) Pour the gin and amaretto into a large glass filled with ice. Stir, then strain into your fancy glass with the absinthe rinse. Garnish with a lemon wedge.

No bones about it, McCoy is not many things, including:

Bartender
Bricklayer
Zookeeper
Psychotherapist
Escalator
Mechanic
Engineer
Magician
Physicist
Torpedo technician
Susan

Klingon Bloodwine

1 part red wine
1 part vodka
1/4 part triple sec
1 part prune juice (a warrior's drink)

Pour all the ingredients into a medium glass filled with ice.

Here are some convenient Klingon toasts for when you enjoy this deep space wine:

'Iwllj jachjaj	*May your blood scream.*
reH HIvje'IljDaq 'Iwghargh Datu' jaj	*May you always find a bloodworm in your glass.*
bltuHpa' blHeghjaj	*Death before shame.*
blSuvtaHvlS blHeghjaj	*May you die in battle.*
Qapla'!	*Success!*

Seven of Wine
ILLUSTRATION BY KATI DELANEY

1 part red wine
1/4 part red Lillet
1/4 part Cognac

Pour all the ingredients into a small, preferably curvy glass filled with ice.

Make It Sloe

Get ready to boss around your crew and see more than four lights when you take command of this cocktail.

3/4 part sloe gin
1/4 part gin
Lemon-lime soda
Soda water

Pour the sloe gin and regular gin into a medium glass filled with ice. Top with half lemon-lime soda and half soda water. Garnish with a lemon wedge.

What's your Picard maneuver?

Jameson T. Kirk

None of us can be as cool as Captain Kirk, but sipping this drink will make you think you are.

1/2 part Jameson whiskey
1/2 part mezcal
1/4 part Cointreau
Ginger beer

Pour the whiskey, mezcal, and Cointreau into a small glass full of ice. Top with ginger beer.

WHAT IS CAPTAIN JAMES T. KIRK'S FAVORITE . . .

Beer: PBR in a KHAN
Film festival: KHANs
Philosopher: KHANt
Country: KHANada
Performer: Chaka KHAN
Line from the movie *The Warriors*: "KHAN you dig it?"
Actor: James KHAN
Melon: KHANtalope
Book: *KHANterbury Tales*
National park: The Grand KHANyon
Vice: KHANabis
Character: KHANibal Lechter
Weapon: KHANnon
Mood: KHANtankerous
Appetizer: KHANapé
Bird: KHANary
Saucy dance: KHAN KHAN
Kitchen implement: KHAN opener
Actress: Madeline Kahn

Kobayashi Maru

1 part homemade gin
1/4 part Bénédictine given to you personally by a Benedictine
    monk
Splash of grenadine
Pineapple juice from the pineapples grown in the Lost Gardens
    of Heligan, near St. Austell, Cornwall, United Kingdom

Hand-chisel a 1-by-1-by-6-inch ice cube from the Kangerlussuaq
glacier in Greenland. Hand-blow a glass that can hold 9.6 ounces
of fluid. While wearing a blindfold, add all the ingredients except
the pineapple juice to a medium glass filled with ice. Top with
pineapple juice.

Takei's Solution

1 part Cognac
1/4 part Cointreau
2 dashes Peychaud's bitters
Splash of lemon juice

Pour all the ingredients into a small glass filled with ice.

Ohhhhh myyyyyy! It's that good.

Uhura's Kiss

1/2 part coffee tequila
1/2 part salted caramel vodka

Pour the ingredients into a large glass filled with ice. Shake or stir, then pour into a small glass, ideally an espresso cup. Twist a lemon peel over the drink and lay it on top.

This drink is a celebration of the first interracial kiss on television, in 1968, between Uhura and Kirk in the episode "Plato's Stepchildren."

It's Okay to Love Both Star Trek and Star Wars

BY PRESIDENT ABRAHAM LINCOLN
(AKA ANDREW MORTON)

"We are not enemies, but friends. We must not be enemies. Though passion may have strained, it must not break our bonds of affection."

Those words were spoken by me as part of my first inaugural address, on the eve of the American Civil War. That war would split the United States apart and turn brother against brother in a brutally violent and wasteful conflict. Today, we are seeing the shadow of a similar conflict arise and harden the hearts of our society, and I, Abraham Lincoln, have once again been called upon to heal the divide. I am, of course, talking about the war between sci-fi fans who think they cannot love both Star Trek and Star Wars at the same time.

You might be surprised that a former president who has been dead since 1865 would have any knowledge of what Star Trek and Star Wars are, but I am intimately familiar with both. So when Andy Heidel called me on the TimePhone I keep inside my stovepipe hat to ask me to again unite our divided nation, I knew I had no choice but to speak out forcefully in the sidebar of a cocktail book.

I will admit, there are certain surface similarities between Star Trek and Star Wars that would invite a kind of one-or-the-other sense of loyalty to the properties. Both series are set in outer space. Both feature larger-than-life heroes who traverse the universe in fast spaceships. And then there's that whole business of each having the word "star" in its title. Since sci-fi nerds are inherently tribalist, it's understandable that they would feel the need to "pick a side," as it were.

But I view things this way: Star Wars, set "a long time ago in a galaxy far, far away," is essentially a fond remembrance of things past. It is a potent mix of mythology and spirituality, suggesting itself as something of a shared, nondenominational origin story of the universe. Star Trek, on the other hand, is all about the future. It offers us a hopeful vision of a time when the Earth is united and war, famine, and poverty have been eliminated. It doesn't just tell us where we are; it shows us where we could boldly go. The past and the future are complementary ideas that allow each series to occupy its own separate ground.

But enough high-mindedness. Why the hell wouldn't I, Abe Lincoln, find both of these series fascinating? Look, as a guy who is often only thought of as being from the past, I'm kind of super-jealous of Star Wars's version of "the olden days." Laser swords? *Millennium Falcons*? Those cool electro-binoculars? If Star Wars takes place in the past, it's one that sucks way less than the past of the 1800s. Trust me—I'm from a time where the most revolutionary technology of the day was the rocking chair. I know that something called a "Death Star" isn't, well, *good,* per se—but all I'm saying is: Lincoln's got himself a Death Star? Then that's one Civil War won inside an hour.

And Star Trek? The aforementioned hopeful vision of future united Earth with no war and poverty? Obviously, that speaks to the president in me. Captain Kirk, a strong leader who must balance his idealism with his pragmatism for the greater good? You're telling me my life story, pal. But if I'm being honest, I'm especially fond of Trek because they let me guest star in the third-season episode "The Savage Curtain" (you remember: the one in which I appear before the *Enterprise* in space, and we arena battle a Klingon and Genghis Khan for the amusement of some rock people). Yeah, it was weird, but if you were assassinated in the prime of your life, you'd be thrilled to have any kind of future at all!

("But Abe," you must be saying, "if you were assassinated many, many decades ago, how could you have been on TV in the 1960s?" It's very complicated, but for the purposes of shorthand, let's just say they *Quantum Leap*-ed me right out of that shit.)

So, from my example, I hope I've shown you that there is no competition between Star Trek and Star Wars, and that you nerds should feel free to enjoy both at the same time. And if some bonehead still can't see the difference between the two, and insists you can't be in two places at once, remind them: Abe Lincoln's already done it, on the U.S. currency: the penny *and* five-dollar bill, baby! Sure, they're both *money,* but they are *just* different enough to not cancel each other out. Mind blown!

And if you still have to fight over it, at least do so in a gentlemanly fashion: over one of the many fine cocktails in this book. I recommend all of them.

May God bless you, the United States of America, Obi-Wan Kenobi, and Mr. Spock.

—Abraham Lincoln

STAR WARS

Sarlacczerac

ILLUSTRATION BY TERESA GALUS

A drink to quench even a desert-level thirst—and it won't take you a thousand years to digest! Perfect for drowning your sorrows over the untimely loss of Boba Fett.

Absinthe
1 orange wedge
1 sugar cube
2 dashes Peychaud's bitters
2 parts Old Overholt rye

Rinse a fancy glass with absinthe. (A rinse is: adding a thimbleful of liquid to your glass first, swirling it around, and pouring out the excess.) Muddle the orange wedge, sugar cube, and bitters in the bottom of a large glass. Add the rye and fill with ice. Stir or shake, then strain into your fancy absinthe-rinsed glass. Make sure to scream as each ingredient enters the maw of your glass.

Leia's Metal Martini
ILLUSTRATION BY ED REYNOLDS

A wishful drink for when you first laid eyes on the bikini-clad Carrie Fisher in Return of the Jedi. *Toast that kid who saw the movie five times in the theater for reasons way more important than the Ewoks. And toast that wonderfully funny, clever woman who was so much more than eye candy.*

1 part Goldschläger
1 part vodka
1/4 part dry vermouth

Pour all the ingredients into a large glass filled with ice. Stir or shake, then strain into a fancy glass.

Blue Milk

By special request. Just what every growing farm boy needs!

1 part blue curaçao
1 part Baileys Irish Cream

Pour the ingredients into a small glass filled with ice.

Thank the Maker's Mark

Okay, did anyone notice that Darth Vader built C-3PO when he was a kid, from scratch? Then that protocol droid got its memory wiped. Throughout the films, whenever he's saved from certain doom, he says, "Thank the maker." He is thanking Darth Vader for his life. Essentially C-3PO is saying, "Praise Satan." Now go grab that bottle of Maker's Mark and mourn your childhood.

John Evan Williams

A symphony of ingredients combine in a drink to score your evening out and make you feel like you have the entire London Symphony Orchestra at your command.

3 mint sprigs
1 part Evan Williams bourbon
Splash of bitters
Lemon-lime soda

Put the mint, bourbon, and bitters in a medium glass filled with ice. Top with lemon-lime soda.

Best accompanied by the following John Williams scores: Star Wars, Jaws, ET, Jurassic Park, Superman, Close Encounters of the Third Kind, Raiders of the Lost Ark, and the first three Harry Potter scores. Play loudly!

Mai Tai Fighter
ILLUSTRATION BY KATI DELANEY

Hard day chasing down rebel scum? Enjoy your shore leave with this classic.

1/2 part Captain Morgan spiced rum
1/2 part Malibu rum
1 part pineapple juice
1 part papaya juice
Splash of orange juice
Splash of grenadine

Pour all the ingredients into a medium glass filled with ice.
Shake or stir. Enjoy.

Millennial Falcon

This drink only works when it wants to.

Degoba Swamp Juice

1/2 part Midori or other melon liqueur
1/2 part vodka
1 part orange juice

All ingredients add to a small glass you will. Filled with ice it will be. Contents of which, stir you will. Drink or do not, there is no try.

Han Shot First

2 shots of your favorite booze
2 bottles of your favorite beer

Not to be enjoyed Solo. We all know who shot first.

STARSHIP TROOPERS

Brain Bug

ILLUSTRATION BY KATI DELANEY

Join the regulars of The Way Station and save the galaxy. Service guaran-
tees a beer stein. Would you like to know more?

Someone asked me once if I knew the difference between a regular and a
barfly. I know now. A regular has the courage to make the safety of the bar
their personal responsibility. A barfly just sits around waiting to see what
happens. Luckily for me, The Way Station is full of regulars.

1 part vodka
1 part Baileys Irish Cream
2 drops grenadine

Pour the vodka first into a shot glass, gently pour the Baileys on top as a float, then add the grenadine.

The Quaffing Dead
with Alissa May Atkinson

Don't be a *Zombie Patron*! Use the brains you still have or at least eat the brains of a smart barfly. This means knowing your order when the bartender asks what you want and having your money or credit card ready to pay. If you are not ready, do not wave the bartender down, or you may be mistaken for the undead. Some *Zombie Patrons* tend to wander away from the bar after ordering, forcing the bartender to hunt them down with a machete. You do not want to be hunted! Be available to complete your transaction. And tipping is not just something Midwestern zombies do to zombie cows. Show your appreciation for the kind service. Beware, your server is not your servant, so be nice and don't bite their head off. Being rude is a surefire way to be ignored, or worse: exiled to the dark and uncertain world beyond the bar doors.

Speaking of doors, do not block the entrance to the bar, bathroom, or any throughway. Barricading doors is reserved for a zombie invasion. Be aware that you are sharing a public area full of mostly nonthreatening humans. Also, please do not take up too much space with your mess. This includes not only whatever fresh kill you may be consuming, but also any of your belongings. All of your personal items should be precious to you with the apocalypse looming so dangerously close. Keep them nearby; they are your responsibility and they will come in handy when you try to fight your way back home. That being said, your most precious possessions are your friends. Look out for them and prevent *Zombie Patrons* from attacking them verbally or physically.

Drinking responsibly is another way to ensure the safety of yourself, belongings, and friends. Be cautious about the speed with which you're consuming and make sure to eat before your night of drinking. Your bartender may offer you a glass of water when you've had a few, so take it and say, "thank you." This not-yet-dead person is a professional and knows what's best for you.

THE WALKING DEAD

Christopher Walken Dead

Hey, we nerds love mash-ups. So don't you think the distinct visage of the great Christopher Walken would make for a fantastic zombie extra on The Walking Dead? *Of course you do! That's one gracefully moving member of the undead.*

Based on the classic Corpse Reviver.

1 part gin
1/4 part absinthe
1/4 part lemon juice

Pour all the ingredients into a large glass filled with ice. Shake or stir, then strain into a fancy glass.

You Will Drink My Energon
BY DEVASTATOR
AS TOLD TO MARC ABBOTT

Deception is the law we live by. You must understand that first if you are to have any dealing with us. It's what fuels us, binds us, controls our decision making. To share food or drink with a Decepticon is, in fact, a deception in and of itself. One would be wise to be careful of what one consumes with us. As I have learned from being around you humans, you all like to live on the edge. So be it.

This drink embodies the very essence of being deceived. A combination of three alcohols with a mixer that goes down smooth and easy like our approach on an Autobot convoy. There lies the deception. Soon after, you will feel the Devastator's kick, which gives off an intense aftertaste that will have you wondering how you ever survived the initial intake.

When you finish, the effects of my concoction coursing through your body will be like electricity from an Energon cube, transforming your desire for bland human cocktails to a need for a drink fit for the greatest five warriors in the universe—me.

Drink up, human!

TRANSFORMERS

Energon

Refuel with this deceptively good drink.

1/4 part blue curaçao
1 part tequila
Tonic water
1/4 part Campari

First, pour the curaçao into a medium glass. Fill the glass with ice, then add the tequila, then pour in tonic water almost to the top. Add the Campari last. You will start off with a cocktail colored like the Autobots, but once you stir it, it transforms into a Decepticon!

Thought for today: If an Autobot has a drink, does that automatically mean he is guilty of drunk driving?

HEIDEL HINT

Bitter Truth. Upset stomach? Drink seltzer or ginger ale with a few dashes of bitters. If you ever have a bad case of hiccups, try a dash of bitters on a lemon wedge with some sugar. Everyone has some silly magic remedy for hiccups. Mine is ridiculous. Ask your hiccupping friend to stare at the ceiling and count down from ten out loud. As they do, rush them by saying, "Faster!" Once they hit one, tell them to say, "Cow, cow, cow." Thirty percent of the time it works every time.

TREMORS

Delirium Tremors

ILLUSTRATION BY TERESA GALUS

Have a bad case of the Graboids? Tread softly and carry a stick of dynamite. This is the ideal cocktail to enjoy on the roof of your trailer while the world burns.

1/4 part Barrow's Intense ginger liqueur or Domaine de
    Canton ginger liqueur
1/4 part Cointreau
6 parts Delirium Tremens beer

Pour the ginger liqueur and Cointreau into a large glass. Top with the beer.

Delirium tremors is a rapid onset of confusion usually caused by withdrawal from Kevin Bacon films.

TRON

RAM

Greetings, Program, I drink for the Users.

1 part dark spiced rum
1 part amaro (works best with Meletti)
1 part mezcal (I suggest Fidencio)

Pour all the ingredients into a medium glass filled with ice. Garnish with a lemon wedge and a quarter.

THE X-FILES

The Vermouth Is Out There
ILLUSTRATION BY ED REYNOLDS

1 part gin
1/2 part sweet vermouth
1/2 part dry vermouth
1/2 part Aperol
Dash of bitters
Splash of lemon

Pour all the ingredients into a large glass filled with ice. Stir, then strain into a fancy glass.

The truth may be out there, but you'll want this drink in you. Do not mix with the black oil!

Smoking Man

Something to drink when you're dans la maison *with no lights on.*

1 part **Dewar's** scotch
1 part mezcal
Splash of lime juice

Pour all the ingredients into a small glass filled with ice. Best sipped slowly with your lips, not through that big hole in your throat.

X-MEN

Cerebroholic

Too many voices in your head? Not enough? Let this libation restore the proper balance in that genius mind of yours. But go easy, Professor—your liver doesn't have a mutant healing factor.

1 part Stoli Salted Karamel vodka
1 part Baileys Irish Cream
1 part Jameson whiskey
4 parts iced coffee

Pour all the ingredients into a large glass filled with ice. Stir with your mind before drinking.

This will break your funk and get you back in the game so you can save the world.

YOUNG FRANKENSTEIN

Abbey Normal
ILLUSTRATION BY ED REYNOLDS

Something amazing and simultaneously terribly wrong.

1 part gin
1/4 part red Lillet
2 parts orange juice
Champagne

Pour the gin, Lillet, and orange juice into a large glass filled with ice. Stir, then strain into a fancy glass and add a Champagne float. Toss a blackberry in so it looks like a tiny brain at the bottom of your glass.

Sweet Mystery of Life

1 part whiskey
1/2 part amaretto
Dash of bitters
Splash of lemon juice

Pour all the ingredients into a small glass filled with ice.

At last I found you.

AFTERWORD

You may have pored (poured?) over this book and wondered why your favorite show, film, character, or catchphrase wasn't included. Unfortunately, unlike the TARDIS, this book contains finite space. So please feel free to contact us at cocktailguidetothegalaxy@gmail.com with your suggestions, and hopefully they'll appear in our follow-up cocktail guides: *The Bar at the End of the Universe* and *Life, the Universe, and Drinking.*

ACKNOWLEDGMENTS

I'd like to thank my family (Mom, Dad, Cat, Lisa, Gail) and my friends Jim Romaine and Olga Losada, without whose contributions I couldn't have opened The Way Station. My forgiving landlord, Eugene Dunning, who didn't evict me when it took two years instead of six months to open and was reasonable when it came to paying the rent. The staff and regulars of The Way Station for their assistance in creating and taste-testing all the recipes in this book. Doc Wasabassco and Andrew Morton for cocktail name generation and invaluable input. Sarah Reidy for her continuous badgering to write this book. Chloé Sehr for keeping me real and editing. Doc for building the TARDIS and Jonathan Fritz for painting the inside mural, which has led to countless press mentions. The bars and incredible bartenders at North Pole, Uncle Barry's, Freddy's, Givers and Takers, Alchemy, and South, where much of this book was written. My agent, Brandi Bowles, at Foundry Literary Agency; my editor, Hannah Braaten; and the whole team at SMP.

And finally I want to thank Douglas Adams, author of *The Hitchhiker's Guide to the Galaxy,* for helping craft my off-kilter sense of humor and inspiring my imagination. I was in my freshman year at the University of Connecticut when he came and gave a lecture and I got to ask him a question about quantum mechanics. I can't remember the exact question, but his response I've never forgotten: "After reading a book on it I passed out on the couch for two days." I think he would appreciate what I've done here.

Qapla'

—Andy Heidel, Brooklyn, New York, June 30, 2016

DRAMATIS PERSONAE

Andy Heidel: Aka Anders, aka Marcie, owner of a nerd bar.

Chloé Sehr: Andy's best friend, storyteller, badass. Aka Sir!

Alissa Atkinson: Seasoned Brooklyn bartender, feisty nugget, says "meow" a lot.

Corey Lange: Pinball wizard, scourge of Fox News.

Doc Wasabassco: Builder of the blue box, burlesque impresario, long-time friend of Anders.

Kati Delaney: Nerd and cocktail savant.

Ed Reynolds: More whiskey than man, longtime friend of Doc and Andy.

Liz Daggar: Creator of TWS logo, further afield agent with Anders.

Teresa Galus: Regular at the bar, designer of three-eyed cats.

Andrew Morton: Everybody's little brother.

Elvis Bob Rasputin: Cocktail connoisseur. Purveyor of meatsweats.

KBRI: Aka Brian Albright, Andy's better half from Pseudo Iguanas fame on WHUS-FM.

Eliza Hecht: "Modern Love" columnist, lady of leisure.

Marc Abbott: Moth grand slam winner, proud father.

Sarah Shanok: Pirate bartender, *Buffy* enthusiast, Steampunky Brewster, Jill-of-all-trades.

Andy Heidel is the owner of The Way Station, a bar and music venue in Brooklyn, NY. As R. Andrew Heidel, he is the author of the short-story collection *Desperate Moon,* which features an introduction by Harlan Ellison and praise from Ray Bradbury. As a book publicist, he launched the Eos imprint and helped make Neil Gaiman, Terry Pratchett, and Neal Stephenson bestselling authors while with Avon Books and HarperCollins. He turned to bar ownership when he was downsized, and hasn't looked back since.